For the christening of

Published by Lion Books
www.lionhudson.com
Part of the SPCK Group
SPCK, 36 Causton Street, London, SW1P 4ST

ISBN 978 0 7459 4778 5

First edition 2002

Acknowledgments
15, 20, 23, 24, 29, 37, 39b, 43a, 43c, 44, 45, 47, 48, 53a, 55, 59b: from the Good News Bible
published by The Bible Societies/HarperCollins Publishers Ltd, UK © American Bible Society
1966, 1971, 1976, 1992, used with permission. 16a, 19, 33, 39a, 43b, 59a, 61: from the *Holy
Bible, New International Version*, copyright © 1973, 1978, 1984 by International Bible Society.
Used by permission. 16b, 25, 31, 35a, 35b, 41, 49, 53b: from The New Revised Standard
Version of the Bible, Anglicized Edition, copyright © 1989, 1995 by the Division of Christian
Education of the National Council of the Churches of Christ in the United States of America,
and used by permission. All rights reserved. 16: 'O Lord', from page 62 of *The Art of Prayer*, Lion
Publishing, 1999. 19, 27: 'Living Lord' and 'Father', from pages 43 and 142 of *365 Children's
Prayers*, Lion Publishing, 1989. 29, 31: 'Christ has died' and The Lord's Prayer in its modern
form, from *The Alternative Service Book 1980*, copyright © The English Language Liturgical
Consultation (ELLC) and reproduced by permission of the publishers. 44: 'Dear God', from
page 92 of *The Lion Book of First Prayers*, Lion Publishing, 1998. 39, 55: 'We have so much' and
'Jesus, who healed the sick', from pages 63 and 102 of *The Lion Treasury of Children's Prayers*, Lion
Hudson, 1999.

Every effort has been made to trace and acknowledge copyright holders of all the quotations in
this book. We apologize for any errors or omissions that may remain, and would ask those
concerned to contact the publishers, who will ensure that full acknowledgment is made in the
future.

Spelling and punctuation of quotations may have been modernized.

A catalogue record for this book is available from the British Library

Printed and bound in China, May 2022, LH54

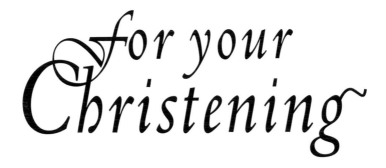

for your Christening

Compiled by
Sarah Medina
Illustrated by
Alexandra Steele-Morgan

LION

Contents

Contents

When I was born

My name ....

My date of birth ....

My time of birth ....

My place of birth ....

My weight ....

My length ....

My eye colour ....

My hair colour ....

How I looked when I was born

When I was christened

Place of christening ....

Date of christening ....

Time of christening ....

Family and friends ....

....

....

....

....

....

....

How I looked when I was christened

When I wake up

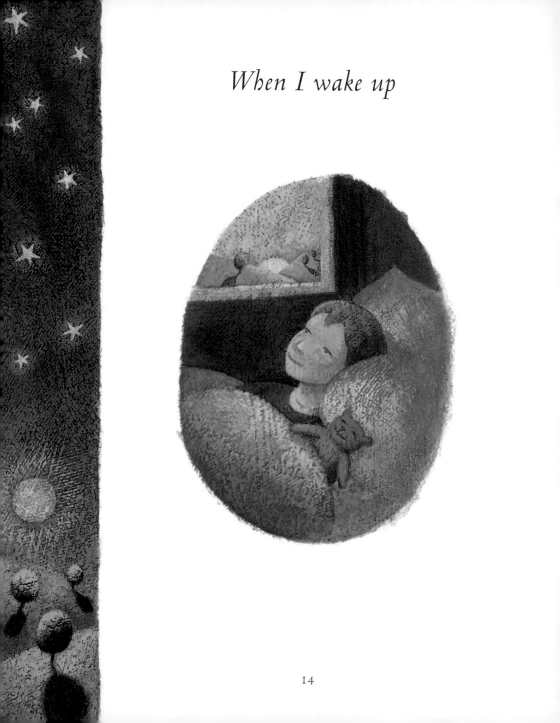

Thank you, God in heaven,
For a day begun.
Thank you for the breezes,
Thank you for the sun.
For this time of gladness,
For our work and play,
Thank you, God in heaven,
For another day.

Traditional prayer

Every day I will thank you;
I will praise you for ever and ever.

Psalm 145:2

For this new morning and its light,
For rest and shelter of the night,
For health and food, for love and friends,
For every gift your goodness sends,
We thank you, gracious Lord.

Author unknown

Dear Lord Jesus,
We shall have this day only once;
before it is gone, help us to do all the good we can,
so that today is not a wasted day.

Stephen Grellet

This is the day the Lord has made;
let us rejoice and be glad in it.

Psalm 118:24

O Lord, into your hands I commit this day.
Be with me at every moment,
keep me from harm,
prompt me to do what is right,
and be what you want me to be.
To your praise and glory.
Amen.

Meryl Doney

The steadfast love of the Lord never ceases,
his mercies never come to an end;
they are new every morning;
great is your faithfulness.

Lamentations 3:22–23

This morning, God,
This is your day.
I am your child,
Show me your way.
Amen.

Author unknown

I open my eyes –
And it's a new day;
Lord, open my eyes –
So I can live it your way.
Amen.

Sarah Medina

Lord, be with us this day.
Within us to purify us;
Above us to draw us up;
Beneath us to sustain us;
Before us to lead us;
Behind us to restrain us;
Around us to protect us.

St Patrick of Ireland

When I play

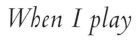

A happy heart makes the face cheerful.

Proverbs 15:13

Loving Father, on this day
Make us happy in our play,
Kind and helpful, playing fair,
Letting others have a share.

The Infant Teacher's Prayer Book

I play:
I walk and I run,
I jump and have fun,
I hop and I skip,
I tumble and trip.
Thank you, dear God,
for watching over me each day.
Amen.

Sarah Medina

The real joy of life is in its play.

Walter Rauschenbach

Living Lord,
Thank you for our hobbies,
and the different things we enjoy.

Carol Watson

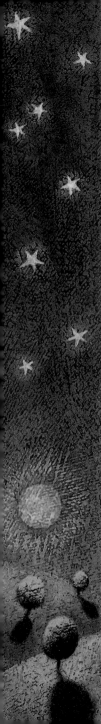

God generously gives us everything for our enjoyment.

I Timothy 6:17

Earth's crammed with heaven.

Elizabeth Barrett Browning

The most wasted day of all is that on which
we have not laughed.

Sebastian R.N. Chamfort

I meant to do my work today –
But a brown bird sang in the apple tree,
And a butterfly flitted across the field,
And all the leaves were calling me.

And the wind went sighing over the land
Tossing the grasses to and fro,
And a rainbow held out its shining hand –
So what could I do but laugh and go?

Richard LeGallienne

Lord, I thank you for making me.
Thank you for all that I can do.
Thank you that I can run, jump, and play games.
Thank you that I can listen to what you tell me.
Thank you that you love me whatever I do.

Andrew (aged 12)

'I have many flowers,' he said, 'but the children
are the most beautiful flowers of all.'

Oscar Wilde

In jumping and tumbling
We spend the whole day,
Till by night arriving
Has finished our play.

What then? One and all,
There's no more to be said,
As we tumbled all day,
So we tumble to bed.

Author unknown

When I learn

The wisest mind has something to learn.

George Santayana

Teach me, my God and King,
In all things thee to see,
And what I do in any thing
To do it as for thee.

George Herbert

Dear God,
Every day I learn something new.
Thank you that the world is so full
of amazing things.
Amen.

Sarah Medina

Guide us, teach us, and strengthen us, O Lord, we beseech
thee, until we become such as thou wouldst have us be:
pure, gentle, truthful, high-minded, courteous, generous,
able, dutiful and useful; for thy honour and glory.

Charles Kingsley

Your word is a lamp to guide me
and a light for my path.

Psalm 119:105

Thank you, Lord, for school.
Thank you that it teaches you to do things.
Lord, please help me to do the best I can
in every single way.
Amen.

Naomi Nicholson (aged 11)

Let this day, O Lord, add some knowledge
or good deed to yesterday.

Lancelot Andrewes

O Lord, bless our school;
That, working together and playing together,
We may learn to serve you
And to serve one another.

A.M. Ammon

Father God,
Thank you for the church and all the teachers.
Thank you that they help us to learn about you.
Please help us to remember what we are taught
And help us to put it into practice.

Alex Foote (aged 12)

Whatever you do, work at it with all your heart.

Colossians 3:23

The things, good Lord, that we pray for,
give us grace to work for;
through Jesus Christ our Lord.

St Thomas More

The fruit of the Spirit is love, joy, peace, patience,
kindness, generosity, faithfulness, gentleness, and
self-control.

Galatians 5:22–23

Teach us, Lord,
to serve you as you deserve,
to give and not to count the cost,
to fight and not to heed the wounds,
to toil and not to seek for rest,
to labour and not to ask for any reward
save that of knowing that we do your will.

St Ignatius Loyola

When I celebrate

My birthday

Dear Father, who hast all things made,
And carest for them all,
There's none too great for thy great love,
Nor anything too small;
If thou canst spend such tender care
On things that grow so wild,
How wonderful thy love must be
For me, thy little child.
G.W. Briggs

Love makes everything lovely.
George Macdonald

Father,
Today it is my birthday.
Please give me a happy day – and also all the other
children in the world who were born on the same day.
Amen.
Carol Watson

Our birthday is the time each year when those around us
celebrate the gift of *us*.
Mike Yaconelli

Christmas

Before the paling of the stars,
Before the winter morn,
Before the earliest cockcrow,
Jesus Christ was born:
Born in a stable,
Cradled in a manger,
In the world his hands had made,
Born a stranger.
Christina Rossetti

It is good to be children sometimes, and never better than
at Christmas, when its mighty founder was a child himself.
Charles Dickens

I heard the bells on Christmas Day
Their old, familiar carols play,
And wild and sweet
The words repeat
Of peace on earth, goodwill to men!
Henry Wadsworth Longfellow

May the Christmas morning make us happy to be your
children and the Christmas evening bring us to our beds
with grateful thoughts.
Robert Louis Stevenson

Easter

Good Friday is a time of sadness,
Easter is a time of gladness.
On Good Friday Jesus died
But rose again at Eastertide.
All thanks and praise to God.
George Macdonald

God loved the world so much that he gave his only Son,
so that everyone who believes in him may have eternal life.
John 3:16

Christ has died:
Christ is risen:
Christ will come again.
The Alternative Service Book

When I pray

Love to pray.

Mother Teresa of Calcutta

Each day is a gift to be opened with prayer.

Author unknown

Our Father in heaven,
hallowed be your name,
your kingdom come,
your will be done,
on earth as in heaven.
Give us today our daily bread.
Forgive us our sins
as we forgive those who sin against us.
Lead us not into temptation
but deliver us from evil.
For the kingdom, the power, and the glory are yours,
now and for ever.
Amen.

The Lord's Prayer

Draw near to God, and he will draw near to you.

James 4:8

Pray often.

John Bunyan

Jesus, friend of little children,
Be a friend to me;
Take my hand and ever keep me
Close to thee.

Never leave me, nor forsake me;
Ever be my friend;
For I need thee, from life's dawning
To its end.

W.J. Mathaus

God be in my head,
And in my understanding;
God be in my eyes,
And in my looking;
God be in my mouth,
And in my speaking;
God be in my heart,
And in my thinking;
God be at my end,
And at my departing.

Traditional prayer

When you can't put your prayers into words,
God hears your heart.

Author unknown

Come into my soul, Lord,
as the dawn breaks into the sky;
let your sun rise in my heart
at the coming of the day.

Traditional prayer

My dearest Lord,
Be thou a bright flame before me,
Be thou a guiding star above me,
Be thou a smooth path beneath me,
Be thou a kindly shepherd behind me,
Today and evermore.

St Columba of Iona

Whatever you ask for in prayer,
believe that you have received it,
and it will be yours.

Mark 11:24

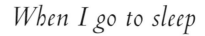

When I go to sleep

I will both lie down and sleep in peace;
for you alone, O Lord, make me lie down in safety.

Psalm 4:8

He gives sleep to his beloved.

Psalm 127:2

Said Day to Night,
'I bring God's light.
What gift have you?'
Night said, 'The dew.'

'I give bright hours,'
Quoth Day, 'and flowers.'
Said Night, 'More blest,
I bring sweet rest.'

Lady Anne Lindsay

Day is done,
Gone the sun
From the lake, from the hills, from the sky.
Safely rest,
All is well!
God is nigh.

Author unknown

Watch, dear Lord,
with those who wake,
or watch, or weep tonight,
and give your angels charge
over those who sleep.
Tend your sick ones, O Lord Christ,
rest your weary ones.
Bless your dying ones.
Soothe your suffering ones.
Pity your afflicted ones.
Shield your joyous ones.
And all for your love's sake.

St Augustine of Hippo

Jesus, tender Shepherd, hear me,
Bless your little lamb tonight;
Through the darkness please be near me,
Watch my sleep till morning light.
All this day your hand has held me,
And I thank you for your care;
You have clothed me, warmed and fed me,
Listen to my evening prayer.
Let my sins be all forgiven;
Bless the friends I love so well;
Take me, when I die, to heaven,
Happy there with you to dwell.

Mary Lundie Duncan

I lie down and sleep, and all night long
the Lord protects me.

Psalm 3:5

God, who made the earth,
The air, the sky, the sea,
Who gave the light its birth,
Careth for me.

God, who made the grass,
The flower, the fruit, the tree,
The day and night to pass,
Careth for me.

God, who made all things,
On earth, in air, in sea,
Who changing seasons brings,
Careth for me.

Sarah Betts Rhodes

When I'm happy

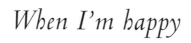

Is anyone happy? Let him sing songs of praise.

James 5:13

We have so much to thank you for,
Our heavenly Father dear:
For life and love and tender care,
Through all the happy year;
For homes and friends and daily food,
Each one a gift of love.
For every good and perfect gift
Is from our God above.

Mary Batchelor

Let us, with a gladsome mind,
praise the Lord, for he is kind;
for his mercies shall endure,
ever faithful, ever sure.

John Milton

When I praise you, Lord,
I feel warm and bubbly inside.
Thank you that I am free to praise you!

Helen Garnham (aged 14)

It is good to sing praise to our God;
it is pleasant and right to praise him.

Psalm 147:1

The world is so full
of a number of things,
I'm sure we should all
be as happy as kings.

Robert Louis Stevenson

Now thank we all our God,
With hearts and hands and voices,
Who wondrous things hath done,
In whom his world rejoices.

Martin Rinckart

How good is the God we adore,
Our faithful unchangeable Friend!
His love is as great as his power,
And knows neither measure nor end!

Joseph Hart

Little deeds of kindness,
Little words of love,
Help to make earth happy,
Like the heaven above.

Julia Carney

Complete happiness is knowing God.

John Calvin

Lord,
Help me to be happy always,
help me to be strong in you,
help me to be well all days,
help me to be good and true.
Amen.

Ruth Hutchinson (aged 7)

Thou that hast given so much to me,
Give one more thing, a grateful heart.

George Herbert

Rejoice in the Lord always;
again I will say, Rejoice.

Philippians 4:4

41

When I'm sad

God says, 'I will comfort you
as a mother comforts her child.'

Isaiah 66:13

Sometimes I feel sad. I don't feel like doing anything
or even talking to anyone. Thank you that you are
with me anyway, God. It reminds me that I am loved.
Amen.

Sarah Medina

Let nothing disturb you,
nothing alarm you:
while all things fade away
God is unchanging.
Be patient
and you will gain everything:
for with God in your heart
nothing is lacking,
God meets your every need.

St Teresa of Avila

Do not grieve, for the joy of the Lord is your strength.

Nehemiah 8:10

Jesus says, 'I will be with you always,
to the end of the age.'

Matthew 28:20

Be near me, Lord Jesus, I ask thee to stay
Close by me for ever, and love me, I pray.
Bless all the dear children in thy tender care;
And fit us for heaven, to live with thee there.

John McFarland

Dear Lord,
When I am sad and alone
I pray to you and then
I am not lonely any more.

Ashley Sturges (aged 12)

Dear God,
Knowing you are with me when I'm sad is like knowing
that the sun is only hidden behind the clouds.
Amen.

Su Box

Jesus says, 'You will not be left all alone.'

John 14:18

God of your goodness, give me yourself,
for you are sufficient for me.
If I were to ask anything less
I should always be in want,
for in you alone do I have all.

Julian of Norwich

I look to the mountains;
where will my help come from?
My help will come from the Lord,
who made heaven and earth.
He will not let you fall;
your protector is always awake.
The protector of Israel
never dozes or sleeps.
The Lord will guard you;
he is by your side to protect you.
The sun will not hurt you during the day,
nor the moon during the night.
The Lord will protect you from all danger;
he will keep you safe.
He will protect you as you come and go
now and for ever.

Psalm 121

When I'm worried

Leave all your worries with God,
because he cares for you.

I Peter 5:7

Alone with none but thee, my God,
I journey on my way.
What need I fear, when thou art near,
O King of night and day?
More safe am I within thy hand
Than if a host did round me stand.

St Columba of Iona

He who would valiant be
'Gainst all disaster,
Let him in constancy
Follow the Master.

John Bunyan

Please, Lord,
Help me to be brave and strong in you,
and take my fear away.
Amen.

Stephen Matthews (aged 13)

Worry is carrying a burden
God never intended us to bear.

Author unknown

What thou shalt today provide,
Let me as a child receive;
What tomorrow may betide,
Calmly to thy wisdom leave.
'Tis enough that thou wilt care;
Why should I the burden bear?

John Newton

Thank you, Lord Jesus, that you will be our hiding place
whatever happens.

Corrie Ten Boom

The Lord is my light and my salvation;
I will fear no one.
The Lord protects me from all danger;
I will never be afraid.

Psalm 27:1

Thank you, Lord, that you reach deep, deep down into
my heart to heal all my worries and hurts.

Susanna Llewellyn (aged 12)

Worry is like a rocking chair.
It'll give you something to do,
but it won't get you anywhere.

Author unknown

The Lord is my shepherd,
I shall not want.
He makes me lie down in green pastures;
he leads me beside still waters;
he restores my soul.
He leads me in right paths for his name's sake.
Even though I walk through the darkest valley,
I fear no evil;
for you are with me;
your rod and your staff — they comfort me.
You prepare a table before me
in the presence of my enemies;
you anoint my head with oil;
my cup overflows.
Surely goodness and mercy shall follow me
all the days of my life,
and I shall dwell in the house of the Lord
my whole life long.

Psalm 23

When I'm cross

For every minute of anger,
you lose sixty seconds of happiness!

Author unknown

I feel so cross, God. I feel cross with everyone
and everything. Please help me to think about you,
God, and about how much you love everyone.
Then maybe I can remember to love them, too,
and my anger can melt away. Thank you.
Amen.

Sarah Medina

Dear Lord,
Sometimes I feel angry.
Please help me to calm my feelings.
Lord, forgive me, because sometimes
I feel angry with you, too.
Amen.

Colin Hiller (aged 9)

Put love into our hearts, Lord Jesus —
love for you;
love for those around us;
love for all we find it hard to like.

Ena V. Martin

Forgive me for the angry words
I didn't mean to say,
Forgive me for the fit of sulks
That spoiled a happy day.
Forgive me for the muddle
That I left upon the floor,
The tea I wouldn't eat,
The hasty way I slammed the door.
Forgive me for my selfishness
And all my little sins,
And help me to be better
When another day begins.

Kathleen Partridge

Never answer an angry word with an angry word.
It's always the second remark that starts the trouble.

Author unknown

The best remedy for anger is a little time for thought.

Seneca

Father,
Make me quick to listen,
but slow to speak,
and slow to become angry.

Based on James 1:19

Thoughtless words can wound as deeply as any sword,
but wisely spoken words can heal.

Proverbs 12:18

Love is patient; love is kind; love is not envious
or boastful or arrogant or rude. It does not insist
on its own way; it is not irritable or resentful;
it does not rejoice in wrongdoing, but rejoices
in the truth.

I Corinthians 13:4–6

Goodness is stronger than evil;
love is stronger than hate;
light is stronger than darkness;
life is stronger than death;
victory is ours through him who loved us.

Desmond Tutu

When I'm unwell

God says, 'I will make you well again.'

Jeremiah 30:17

Jesus, who healed the sick,
Be with me in my pain;
Please help me to be brave
And make me well again.

Mary Batchelor

Lord, hang on to me,
because I don't feel well enough
to hang on to you.

Angela Ashwin

I'm tired, Lord, but I'll lift one foot
if you'll lift the other for me.

Sadie Patterson

I feel awful, Lord. I hate feeling so unwell.
Please help me to get better soon.
Help me to remember to be thankful to you
at all times – even now.
Amen.

Sarah Medina

Lord, let me make sickness itself a prayer.

St François de Sales

O God, grant me courage, gaiety of spirit
and tranquillity of mind.

Robert Louis Stevenson

In sorrow and suffering, go straight to God
with confidence, and you will be strengthened,
enlightened and instructed.

St John of the Cross

O Jesus,
Be the canoe that holds me up
in the sea of life;
Be the rudder that keeps me
on a straight course;
Be the outrigger that supports me
in times of great temptation.
Let your Spirit be my sail
that carries me through each day.
Keep my body strong, so I can paddle
steadfastly on in the voyage of life.

Islander's prayer from Melanesia

May he be blessed for ever
who has taken such care of me.

St Teresa of Avila

We cannot fall beneath the arms of God.
However low we fall,
they are still underneath us.

William Penn

Drop thy still dews of quietness
Till all our strivings cease;
Take from our souls the strain and stress,
And let our ordered lives confess
The beauty of thy peace.

Breathe through the heats of our desire
Thy coolness and thy balm;
Let sense be dumb, let flesh retire;
Speak through the earthquake, wind and fire,
O still small voice of calm!

John Greenleaf Whittier

When I'm peaceful

The Lord blesses his people with peace.

Psalm 29:11

May the Lord bless you and take care of you;
May the Lord be kind and gracious to you;
May the Lord look on you with favour and give you peace.

Numbers 6:24–26

Deep peace of the running wave to you;
Deep peace of the flowing air to you;
Deep peace of the quiet earth to you;
Deep peace of the shining stars to you;
Deep peace of the gentle night to you.
Moon and stars pour their healing light on you;
Deep peace of Christ the light of the world to you;
Deep peace of Christ.

Celtic prayer

Peace is always beautiful.

Walt Whitman

O Lord my God,
grant us your peace; already, indeed,
you have made us rich in all things!
Give us that peace of being at rest...
the peace that knows no end.

St Augustine of Hippo

Still, very still.
Now I am ready for hearing God.
Now I am ready for listening.
Now I am ready to talk to him.
Still, very still.

Author unknown

The lightning and thunder
They go and they come;
But the stars and the stillness
Are always at home.

George Macdonald

I will not hurry through this day!
Lord, I will listen by the way,
To humming bees and singing birds,
To speaking trees and friendly words;
And for the moments in between
Seek glimpses of thy great Unseen.

I will not hurry through this day;
I will take time to think and pray;
I will look up into the sky,
Where fleecy clouds and swallows fly:
And somewhere in the day, maybe
I will catch whispers, Lord, from thee!

Ralph Spaulding Cushman

Christ be with me, Christ within me,
Christ behind me, Christ before me,
Christ beside me, Christ to win me,
Christ to comfort and restore me.
Christ beneath me, Christ above me,
Christ in quiet and Christ in danger,
Christ in hearts of all that love me,
Christ in mouth of friend and stranger.

St Patrick of Ireland

All is silent.
In the still and soundless air,
I fervently bow
To my almighty God.

Hsieh Ping-hsin

Be still, and know that I am God.

Psalm 46:10